BLOOM

BLOOM

A Woman's Journal for Inspired Living

By Lynne Franks

CHRONICLE BOOKS

SAN FRANCISCO

ISBN-10: 0-8118-5755-7
ISBN-13: 978-0-8118-5755-0

Design by Suzanne LaGasa
Manufactured in China
Chronicle Books endeavors to use environmentally
responsible paper in its gift and stationery products.

Distributed in Canada by
Raincoast Books
9050 Shaughnessy Street
Vancouver, British Columbia V6P 6E5

10 9 8 7 6 5 4 3 2 1

Chronicle Books LLC
680 Second Street
San Francisco, California 94107
www.chroniclebooks.com

Dedication and Gratitude

I wrote *Bloom* not only for all the wonderful women of the world, but also for my little granddaughter Lola Mae Catto, my goddaughter India Rose Catto, and all the future grandchildren. I am so grateful for the joy and delight they bring into my life, and I promise that, alongside the other grandmothers, I will use my experience and wisdom to light the way for generations to come.

I would like to honor my writing companion and friend Michael Bockman for his wise contribution. I would also like to thank Carey Jones of Chronicle Books for her support and encouragement. Together we planted the seeds for *Bloom* over lunch in San Francisco, resulting in the flowering of what we both believe to be an inspirational tool for women everywhere.

INTRODUCTION

As women, we are looking for the key to true happiness in a rapidly changing world. We no longer expect to live the lives of our mothers and grandmothers, who knew what their futures might hold. We live in a time of such diverse opportunities and uncertainty that we can sometimes feel isolated or trapped by our insecurities.

Bloom presents you with a map that will help guide you through your life's journey. By completing the stimulating exercises in this unique journal – a sort of workshop in a book – followed by reflective journaling, you will experience a period of major growth, clearing the weeds from the garden of your life, sowing seeds in the form of new ideas and fresh inspiration, and tending to those ideas through your actions. *Bloom* will enable you to discover new insights into yourself so that you might design your life's garden based on your true passions, desires, and goals. And when your flowers finally begin to blossom, you will be living in the garden of your dreams.

As a successful businesswoman in the 1980s, a single mother in the '90s, and now an author and teacher in the twenty-first century, I have learned how important it is to develop my conscious awareness so that I can experience the fulfillment and connection that I've always yearned for. I have discovered how I lived in denial for many years, juggling all my responsibilities at such a speed that I never stopped for breath. Only after my life came crashing down around my ears in the early 1990s—when my marriage unexpectedly came to an end, I experienced career burnout, and my health started to suffer—did I realize how lucky I was to be alive.

By stopping to experience the pause between breaths, by honoring all the beautiful gifts that Mother Nature continually offers us, by appreciating the love I felt from my children and friends, and by understanding that by slowing down I could actually make a greater contribution in the long run, I started to discover my true identity.

I decided to live my life in a way that fully supported my soul. I sold my successful PR agency and began my personal journey. I studied different cultures and beliefs, listened to the stories of others, and discovered how to connect with myself from a place of love.

What I've learned from the women I've talked with all over the world is that there is a universal desire to find fulfillment within oneself rather than in the trappings of what is traditionally thought of as a "good life." Women are coming to understand, as I did, that slowing down and looking within to discover their feminine core can bring unimaginable growth and happiness.

To get the most out of this journal, pay special attention to the exercises that really resonate with you. Some of the exercises are easy to do, while some take effort; some are meant to be fun, while others require you to dig deep within yourself. There is no need to do them in the exact order presented, but try to do them all, for they all offer some illumination. If an exercise strikes a distinct chord with you, you may want to photocopy and repeat it. You can also use the blank pages at the very end of the journal to go into more detail on certain exercises.

After completing this journal, you, too, will be able to experience the flowering of your consciousness. You will be able to construct a new vision of your life based on what truly matters to you: personal growth, well-being, relationships, work, and contribution. Ultimately, *Bloom* will help you focus on being fully aware and alive in every moment, connecting with yourself and those in your life, and nurturing yourself so that you can become all you were born to be.

See you in the garden,

PERSONAL
GROWTH

Chapter 1

PERSONAL GROWTH

Women today want more. Having careers, relationships, families, possessions—all those things we were told would lead to happiness—has instead left many of us thirsting for the one thing we've yet to acquire: personal fulfillment. The exercises in this section are designed to help you achieve that fulfillment by embarking on a journey of personal growth, finding out who you really are, and learning how to get in touch with your feminine essence.

This journey can be challenging, but it also provides the opportunity to open yourself up to transformation, letting go of your personal blocks and fears. There are passions to find, triumphs to experience, quiet wells of peace to explore, rich veins of power to tap into, freedom to discover, and, ultimately, dreams to achieved.

It is important when doing these exercises to be as open and honest as you can with yourself. As when planting a garden, the soil needs to be unsettled before a seed can germinate. Often there are deeper thoughts and emotions behind the first answer that pops into your head. Don't be afraid to travel to those great unexplored areas within yourself.

In the sixth exercise in this chapter you will be asked to create an affirmation. An affirmation is a declaration to the universe communicating a specific wish or prayer, or a simple offer of gratitude. An example of an affirmation I like came to me from the great Nigerian musician Babatunde Olatunji: "May only that of the greatest and highest good come to me today."

1. I Take Off My Mask and Show the Beauty Within

Now is the time to reveal your true self in all your splendor. The roles that we take on—partner, employee, daughter, friend, mother—can often obscure the magical feminine soul within. It is time to reconnect with the beauty of the inner you, who lives with complete authenticity and shines like a radiant sun.

Taking Off the Mask

Put on your makeup as if you were going to work. Once you are finished, look in the mirror for three minutes, then write in detail what you saw reflected in the mirror.

....

....

....

....

....

....

....

....

Now use your makeup to put on your "party" face. Once again, gaze in the mirror for three minutes and then record your observations.

....

....

....

....

....

....

....

....

Finally, with or without makeup, gaze into the mirror to find the woman that is the real you. Then answer the question, "Who am I?"

Examples:
I am a dancer
I am a leader
I am a gardener
I am a vibrant, beautiful woman

I am ....

I am ....

I am ....

I am ....

....

....

2. I Make the Space and Time to Stay in Tune with My Higher Self

We live in a world where being busy is the norm. So much of our lives is taken up with things to do that we often forget how joyful it is just to *be*. Taking quiet time and completely calming your mind, if only for a few minutes each day, is the best gift you can give yourself. It is in this pool of tranquility that you will find all the answers you will ever need.

Finding My Quiet Place

Find a quiet area in your house or garden and take nothing with you but yourself. Get as comfortable as you can, leaving your eyes open or closed, depending on your preference. Breathe regularly. As you relax every muscle in your body, imagine a beam of light coming from the space between your eyes, connecting you with your higher energy.

Become more relaxed with each calming breath. As you go deeper, ask only for connection with your true self. Whatever your belief system, there is help available to you from the highest part of your being, which is there to guide you.

Remain open to whatever thoughts or emotions arise, embracing the wisdom of your inner voice. Don't be afraid to linger in this luminous place. When you are ready, slowly bring your senses back to the present space around you.

Now write about the experience you have just had.

....
....
....
....
....
....
....
....
....
....
....
....
....
....
....

HIGHER Self

MAKE the Space and TIME to Stay in TUNE with my?

Make a commitment to do this exercise for at least seven consecutive days. You'll find that the more you do it, the easier it becomes and the more it replenishes your body and spirit.

3. I Plant Seeds As Well As Pick Blooms

All new beginnings must start with the conscious planting of "seeds" in your life's garden: your passions, your interests, and your dreams. Planting seeds is about becoming aware of what is important to you and what fills you with deep satisfaction.

My Passions

When I was a child, I always played . . .

....

....

....

....

....

When I was a teenager, I used to spend my time . . .

....
....
....
....

When I became an adult, my biggest passions were . . .

....
....
....
....

Now list twenty activities that light up your soul.

....
....
....
....
....
....
....
....
....
....

Are your passions incorporated in your work and play today? If not, how can you bring
them into your life now?

....
....
....
....
....

4. I Never Let Go of the Big Vision

Now that you've identified some "seeds" that you'd like to plant, it's time to map out your garden.

My Vision Poster

On a large piece of poster board, attach a picture of yourself looking happy and strong at the top center. At the very center of the board, paste an image of the great universal power, however you imagine it. It could be a picture of a religious figure or goddess, it could be a mystical symbol, or it could be an image of pure golden light. Next, add to your Vision Poster images of your loved ones: your partner, relatives, children, and friends.

Now, find images from old magazines or books that illustrate a passion, profession, skill, wish, or place—in fact, anything that resonates with you—and add them to your poster. Follow your intuition, and allow your inner self to guide the images you use and where you place them. Have fun with it; make it as artful as you wish.

Don't stop there. Pick up a marker and write down some of the "seeds" you listed in the previous exercise. Let the collage take shape in a spontaneous fashion. Almost magically, an insightful picture of yourself embodying your passions, dreams, and path will appear.

When finished, write about what you see on your poster.

Through the coming weeks and months, keep this poster in a place where you can see it, and keep adding to it as the inspiration strikes. You can also photograph your poster at different stages and paste it in the space provided on the following pages. You'll be surprised how enriching this image of your life's garden can be.

My Vision Poster

[Photo Here]

My Vision Poster

[Photo Here]

5. I Open My Heart and Surrender to the Vital Flow of the Universe

There is a miraculous universal force that, when tapped, seems to give us all the power and direction we need. We have all felt its golden light, when all was right with the world and every choice, action, and step we took was absolutely perfect.

Surrendering is about giving up our need to control results and, instead, creating a purity of intention, trusting that the universal force will give us exactly what we need. When we let go in this way, good things almost always happen.

Letting Go

A time in my past when I tried to control the outcome was . . .

....
....
....
....

The ultimate outcome was . . .

....
....
....
....

A time when I surrendered and let the outcome happen naturally was . . .

....
....
....
....

When I let go of my attachment to the outcome I felt . . .

....
....
....
....
....

The ultimate outcome when I let go and surrendered was . . .

....

....

....

....

A future outcome I wish to come to pass is . . .

....

....

....

....

....

I can put myself in a position to make it happen while also surrendering to the ultimate outcome the universe gives me by . . .

....

....

....

....

....

....

....

....

....

....

....

....

....

....

....

....

....

OPEN my ♥ Heart AND SURRENDER TO THE VITAL FLOW OF THE Universe

6. I Manifest Abundance in All Areas of My Life

We can experience abundance not just with respect to material things: It can also be experienced in our relationships, our play, our food, our health, and our spirit. The first step to manifesting abundance is to see the richness in your life now. Bringing dreams to fruition comes from realizing that all manifestations are gifts from the Creator. To manifest abundance you must clearly set your intention, open your heart, and surrender to what the universe provides.

Manifesting Abundance

Three things I am grateful for are . . .

....

....

....

....

These things came into my life when . . .

....

....

....

....

....

....

I would currently like to manifest . . .

....

....

....

....

....

....

....

....

....

Create and write down an affirmation that you will say every day to turn this
desire into reality.

....

....

....

....

....

....

....

Remember: The universe has many surprises in store, and the form
your manifestation takes may surprise you. Accept its gifts with
open arms.

7. I Acknowledge the Goddess Within Me

The Goddess is another name for the sacred feminine energy within each of us, and is your highest state of being. To be in your full power—happy, confident, and connected with the universe—it is essential to reclaim the Goddess spirit that stirs inside of you. Your inner Goddess is always there at the ready, so call her whenever you need her.

Finding the Goddess

Recall a specific time in your past when you felt like a Goddess—completely in your power. How old were you? What were you doing? Where were you? What happened?

....

....

....

....

....

....

....

....

....

....

....

....

....

....

....

....

....

....

....

....

....

....

Now close your eyes and, using the relaxation techniques you learned in exercise 2, begin to see and feel that extraordinary time you were in your Goddess power. What are the voices and sounds around you? What does it smell like? Is it warm, hot, cold, or cozy? How does your body feel? Strong? Limber? Supple? How does your spirit feel? Powerful? Light? Indulge yourself in this sumptuousness.

As you bring yourself back to the present, name that time you experienced your Goddess power—a Goddess name like Athena or Shakti—in order to anchor it in your memory, so that, when you say that Goddess's name again, it will instantly help you relive that glorious moment.

Write about the experience you've just had and name your Goddess.

....

....

....

....

....

....

....

....

....

....

....

....

....

....

....

....

....

....

....

....

....

....

....

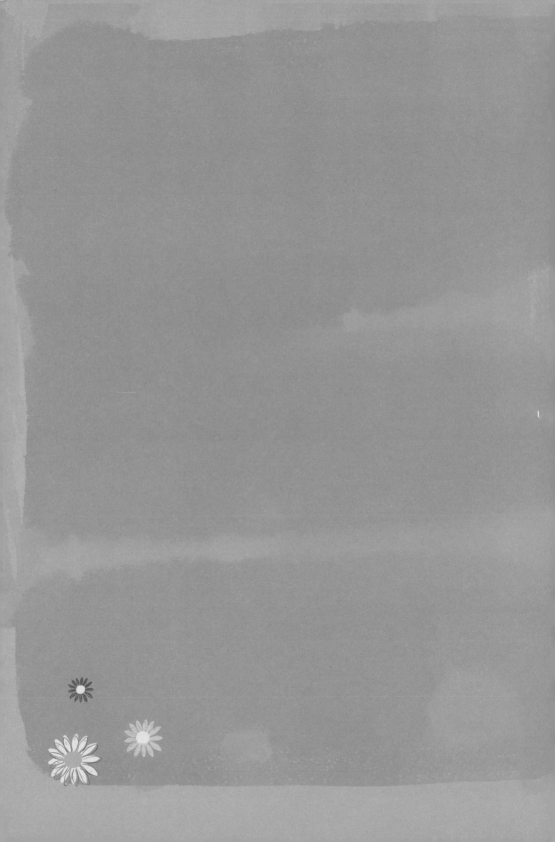

WELL-BEING

Chapter 2

WELL-BEING

One of the greatest challenges we face as women is balancing the three pillars of well-being: body, mind, and spirit. In order to live your life to the fullest, it is essential that these three aspects of your well-being work in harmony.

We can begin by learning to love and connect with our bodies. The first step for many of us is to stop believing what the media says we should look like and allow ourselves to celebrate what we do look like.

The exercises in this chapter are meant to bring awareness to all your habits related to your well-being and show you how easily they can be improved. When it comes to food, for example, it's not necessary to regularly deny yourself, but, rather, to be aware of what you eat and to learn how to eat healthily. Similarly, physical exercise doesn't have to be a chore if you find activities that allow you have fun while you get in shape.

Along with your body, it is equally important that your mind and spirit are as healthy as they can be. If you feel you're in a rut, if life is not as exciting or rewarding as you would like, perhaps it is time to see things with a fresh perspective. Break out, change your habits, see the sunrise, hear the birds sing, smell the flowers, and experience the beauty and inspiration that surrounds you.

Embracing your well-being is honoring your body as the divine gift it is and feeling the exhilarating freedom that every new day brings.

8. I Make Every Day My Birthday

Are you filled with joy when you open your eyes every morning? Do you look forward to the opportunities of the day ahead? Every new sunrise gives birth to new life. So celebrate!

My Birthday Party

One special birthday that gave me supreme joy was . . .

....

....

....

....

The circumstances that made it special were . . .

....

....

....

....

One special birthday present I'll always remember was . . .

....

....

....

....

Upon waking tomorrow, light a candle and declare it your birthday. Think of a gift you would like to give yourself—it could be anything from a new dress to a massage to a simple flower to a walk in a beautiful garden—and then make it happen.

Gifts, large or small, that I can give myself every day for the next week are . . .

....

....

....

....

....

....

....

....

....

....

....

....

....

....

....

....

....

Now actually give yourself these daily gifts as a reminder that every day is your birthday. Make the special effort, because you are worth it!

9. I Get Up Early in the Morning

Morning time has a vibrant energy all its own. By starting your day early, you become infused with the vitality the new dawn brings. Your energy will be higher, your powers of concentration better, and your ability to tap into your consciousness deeper. By starting your day in the calm of the morning, you will be able to set the tone for your entire day.

Making the Morning Glorious

For one week, set your alarm an hour earlier than usual. Use this time exclusively as *your* time, doing the things you don't have the time for later in the day. Meditate, stretch, or take a luxurious bath or a morning walk.

Use at least fifteen minutes of your hour to write in your journal, spontaneously writing whatever comes to mind. Dreams, ideas, and insights arise from your subconscious when you let your pen flow freely over the page. Don't think, just write.

GET UP EARLY

in the Morning

If waking up an hour earlier initially leaves you tired, try moving your bedtime up an hour. Although this may seem like an effort at first, you'll quickly begin to appreciate the rewards the early morning offers.

10. I Remember My Body Is My Most Important Tool

Are you as healthy as you could be? Do you put self-care on the back burner? Keeping your body fit is essential for maintaining a healthy balance in life. When your body feels good, your mind, emotions, and spirit are able to soar.

Physical activity should be a pleasure, not a chore. It can bring you endless fun and fulfillment if you find activities you enjoy. There are so many rewarding ways to get your exercise, including walking, dancing, yoga, gardening, Pilates, stretching, karate, jogging, bicycling, swimming, skating, t'ai chi, tennis, and team sports.

Joys of the Body

Ten activities I enjoy doing are . . .

....

....

....

....

....

....

....

....

....

....

From this list, create an activity schedule for at least one week. Do at least one activity every day, trying a different activity each time. Don't be overly ambitious, though: The most important thing is just to do something, even if it's stretching for five minutes at the office.

I will .... on Monday.

I will .... on Tuesday.

I will .... on Wednesday.

I will .... on Thursday.

I will .... on Friday.

I will .... on Saturday.

I will .... on Sunday.

Every day, write about what activity you did, how it made you feel, and if it was enjoyable.

Monday...

....

....

....

Tuesday...

....

....

....

Wednesday...

....

....

....

Thursday..

....

....

....

Friday..

....

....

....

Saturday..

....

....

....

Sunday..

....

....

....

After the first week, create a new exercise schedule. Include only activities you enjoyed doing. Make a goal of exercising at least four times a week. Keep at it: Once you get into the habit of exercising, you'll be surprised how easily it becomes part of your daily routine.

I will ....
....
.... on Monday.

I will ....
....
.... on Tuesday.

I will ....
....
.... on Wednesday.

I will ....
....
.... on Thursday.

I will ....
....
.... on Friday.

I will ....
....
.... on Saturday.

I will ....
....
.... on Sunday.

Remember My body is my most IMPORTANT tool

Go for a walk

STRETCH EXERCISE

Breathe

DANCE

11. I Drink Six to Eight Glasses of Water a Day and Maintain a Nutritious Diet

If exercise is one of the main pillars of a healthy life, a healthy diet is another. Our bodies are more than two-thirds water. We lose water every moment we are alive, so it is essential for our health to properly rehydrate with at least six to eight glasses of water a day.

Similarly, the food we eat is the fuel our body burns. What do you put in your tank? Premium fuel or low-grade junk? Your body can always feel the difference.

Strict diets rarely work over the long term. Becoming aware of what you eat, how much, and how your body reacts is the ultimate secret to a healthy diet. Conscious eating is healthy eating.

My Eating Habits: The Good, the Bad, and the Ugly

Take two weeks for this exercise. For the first week, write down everything you consume, including meals, snacks, beverages, cigarettes, alcohol, and sweets. Write about how it makes your body feel. How is your energy? Do you feel achy or bloated?

Week One

Monday

Tuesday

Wednesday

Thursday

Friday

Saturday

Sunday

For the second week, eat and drink a healthy diet, balancing your intake of protein, complex carbohydrates, and vegetables; reducing sweets, caffeine, and alcohol; and drinking plenty of water. Write down what you've consumed this week, and take note of how your body feels.

Week Two

Monday ....
....
....
....
....
....

Tuesday ....
....
....
....
....
....

Wednesday ....
....
....
....
....
....

Thursday ....
....
....
....
....

Friday ....

Saturday ....

Sunday ....

By eating consciously and moderately, you can remain fit and healthy for a lifetime!

DRINK 6 to 8 GLASSES OF PURE WATER EVERY DAY

12. I Keep Humor and Laughter As Vital Ingredients in My Life

Stress, tension, anxiety, worry, fear, pressure, problems, doubt, obstacles, anguish, pain, sorrow: These are all good reasons we need as much laughter as we can muster. Life is serious business—sometimes it can get a little too serious. Humor puts difficult things into perspective. The ability to take a step back and see humor in stressful situations can often relieve tension and defuse frustration or anger. Maintaining good humor enhances health, creates goodwill, helps us maintain a positive attitude, and, most importantly, makes life a lot more fun.

Finding the Humor

Write about a time when you used humor to help ease a stressful or difficult situation.

Keep HUMOR and LAUGHTER as vital ingredients in my LIFE

Experiencing Laughter

Scientific studies have shown that the physical act of laughter is one of the most healthy behaviors we humans can engage in. It helps to relieve stress and lower blood pressure and enables the body to release an array of beneficial hormones. Experience the pure, wonderful sensation of laughter. Find an area or room where you can shed any self-consciousness, then bring yourself to laugh. Start with a chuckle and build to a belly laugh. As you laugh, be aware of all the sensations within your body and how wonderfully relaxing and liberating laughter can be.

13. I Appreciate the Beauty Around Me Every Day

Bringing beauty and inspiration into our lives is as important as keeping our bodies well tuned. Our hearts continually need lifting, and our souls need to be nourished with inspiration. The miraculous beauty of life is all around you. Read a poem, listen to an inspiring piece of music, look at a wonderful painting, take a walk into nature. If you remain open to beauty, the world will inspire you in unexpected ways.

Opening to Inspiration

Write a poem or some prose about something that has inspired you. Don't think too hard or try to be brilliant; just follow your inspiration and let the words flow.

14. I Learn the Rules, and Then Break Some

Breaking rules is about consciously changing patterns so we don't get stuck in our routines. When we begin living our lives by rote, we often stop moving forward. It's important to continually examine why we act the way we do. Questioning our actions and beliefs often leads to breakthroughs and new, rewarding ways to live—at work, at home, and in the world. Our well-being requires that we occasionally challenge our behaviors and break some rules and patterns that restrict us. Doing so allows us to see life with fresh eyes and act with a new sense of freedom.

Breaking Free

A routine or behavior I would like to change is . . .

....
....
....
....

I'd like to change this routine or behavior because . . .

....
....
....
....
....
....
....

I could responsibly change this routine or behavior by . . .

....
....
....
....
....
....
....

Go ahead and change your routine or break the rule, and then write about what happened when you did. How did it make you feel? Was breaking this rule or changing this pattern significant to you?

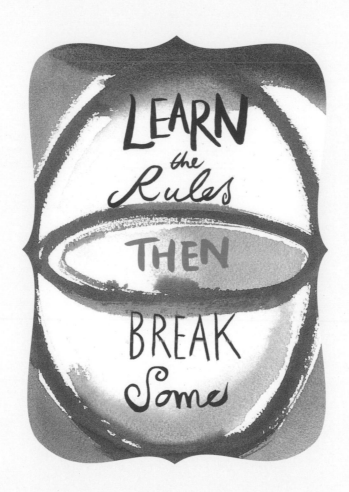

RELATIONSHIPS

Chapter 3

RELATIONSHIPS

We experience two types of relationships: the one we have with ourselves and those we have with others. The mastery of both is key to a happy life.

Relationships are particularly important for women. We need interaction, communication, support, understanding, and empathy from others and from ourselves. The exercises in this section are designed to help you examine the nature of your relationships, find your feminine power within, and then connect with others as a strong, confident woman.

Learning to deepen all of our connections is often a matter of becoming more aware of the way we use our social skills. Can we be more attentive with people? Do we listen closely? Do we always say what we mean? Are we reaching out to others? Being a conscious connector is essential for building solid relationships.

At the heart of all relationships, especially intimate ones, is trust. Trust is built by creating a foundation of truth. When awareness and truth are brought to relationships, new levels of intimacy and connection can be achieved with colleagues, friends, and lovers.

15. I Know Nothing is More Sexy Than Confidence

We are all beautiful. The problem is that we often have trouble believing it. Low self-esteem runs rampant among women. Even those who seem most confident are often plagued with doubts about themselves.

We all come in different sizes, shapes, and colors. The key to real confidence is realizing the wonderful uniqueness each one of us brings to the world. Once you get in touch with the exquisite soul inside you, your confidence will radiate like a sparkling diamond.

Recognizing My Beauty

Five wonderfully unique things about me are . . .

....

....

....

....

....

Five of my most attractive physical features are . . .

....

....

....

....

....

Five things about my personality that are special are . . .

....

....

....

....

....

Five ways I can begin to embrace the positive aspects of myself, leaving the negative behind, are . . .

....
....
....
....
....
....
....
....

16. I Celebrate the Mystery and Pleasure of My Sexuality

One of the joys of being a woman is being in touch with the mystery of our sexuality. Our sexuality is not just the passion unleashed around sex itself; it's an energy we carry and can connect with at any time. Our sexuality is unlimited and abundant. It is the Goddess inside every woman. Don't be afraid to unleash it!

The Pleasure Zone

Think of a wild fantasy or an erotic poem, then write it down in as much wonderful detail as you can. You never have to show it to anyone, but don't be shy about visiting it when needed.

....

....

....

....

....

....

....

....

....

....

....

....

....

....

....

....

....

....

....

....

....

Celebrate the MYSTERY and Pleasure of my Sexuality

17. I Believe in Myself, So Others Will Too

Living up to your true potential takes courage, and, unfortunately, we are often held back by our self-doubts and fears. Women frequently have a fear of being seen, and often we fear confrontation. Some of us fear being alone, and others fear opening their hearts and becoming vulnerable. Repeat this mantra to yourself when you feel fearful: Fear is a paper tiger when faced.

You might be surprised how often you face your fears with courage in your daily life and don't give yourself credit. Whether it's speaking up in public, driving in heavy traffic, or being truthful with a friend, we all act courageously every day.

Facing My Fears

What do you fear most?

....

....

....

....

....

Why is it your greatest fear?

....

....

....

....

....

....

....

Visualize yourself facing that fear. Write about the experience.

....

....

....

....

....

....

....

....

....

Create your own mantra or affirmation of your positive self-beliefs and repeat it every time you're feeling afraid.

....

....

....

....

....

....

....

....

....

18. I Make Truth the Foundation of All My Relationships

The truth really does set you free, because honesty builds openness and trust, and living a life of integrity offers abundant rewards. Take a close look at why you do or say things. Are you always entirely truthful with others and with yourself?

The Honest Truth

One occasion when I wasn't completely honest, either with others or myself, was . . .

....

....

....

....

....

....

....

....

....

....

....

The reasons I wasn't completely honest were . . .

....

....

....

....

....

....

....

....

....

....

I, ... , affirm that it is my intention
to come from a place of honesty at all times and establish truth and integrity as the
foundation of all my relationships.

Signed ....

Dated ....

19. I Listen As Well As Talk

Listening is a skill we can all improve. A conversation becomes more fulfilling when we listen with complete attention rather than thinking about what we are going to say next. We are also more likely to perceive the insights the speaker has to offer. Good listeners are almost always well liked, because they offer the gift of genuine human connection.

Learning to Listen

How do I listen in a conversation?

....

....

....

....

....

....

....

....

....

What would the benefits be if I were a better listener?

....

....

....

....

....

....

....

....

....

....

....

....

Next time you are participating in a conversation, pay attention to how you listen. Become conscious of the inner dialogue that goes on in your head. Try and repeat the speaker's words inside your head as they talk. Then write about the experience and what difference it made in the way you listened and heard.

20. I Talk Slowly But Think Quickly

Listening with attention is complemented by being mindful when you speak. "Talking slowly" doesn't necessarily require slowing down your speech, but, rather, involves speaking from a place of awareness. We've all said something we wish we could take back, whether in the heat of an argument, in casual conversation, or when we gossip. Next time you're in conversation, stop for a moment and reflect on if you are really present to what you are saying. Let your words come from thoughtfulness.

Speaking with Awareness

An occasion when I spoke too quickly and got myself into trouble was . . .

....

....

....

....

....

....

If I had paused to reflect, how would I have spoken differently?

....
....
....
....
....
....
....
....
....

How might the situation have turned out differently?

....
....
....
....
....
....
....
....

Return to this page when you have paused in a conversation and chosen to speak from a more thoughtful place. Write about the experience and how the increased awareness of your speech made a difference.

....
....
....
....
....
....
....
....
....

21. I Do Not Neglect My Loved Ones or Friends in Any Way

What makes your life worthwhile? Your work? Your relationships? Your family? Your play time? The answer is all of them, of course, and that is why it is so important to create a balance between all aspects of your life.

If you find yourself so entangled in your career or caught up with the details of life that quality time with your family and friends suffers, it's time to rebalance things. There's no better time than now to share love and support with a friend.

Reaching Out

Choose someone you want to communicate something important to. Draft a letter here, and then read it aloud. Once you are satisfied with it, copy it onto nice stationery and send it. The reward will be yours.

....

....

....

....

....

....

....

....

....

....

....

....

....

....

....

....

....

....

....

Do not neglect my personal relationships, loved ones and friends in any way

WORK

Chapter 4

WORK

Because work plays such a central role in our lives, it is essential to create a work atmosphere that allows us to flourish as women while earning our livelihoods. Traditional offices are often functional, logical, hierarchical, non-nurturing places. Although these traits are not inherently bad, they devalue many of the innate talents that women bring to the workplace. We are good at relationship building, communicating, networking, multitasking, nurturing, and exercising intuition, compassion, and empathy.

By bringing your feminine talents, values, and aesthetics to your job, you can begin to transform yourself as well as improve your office environment so that it nurtures and reflects your capabilities and is a more pleasurable place for you to work.

The rules of the workplace are not that different from the rules that apply to everyday life. How you deal with the obstacles and difficulties you face every day—whether you allow them to defeat you or use these challenges as opportunities to learn and grow personally and professionally— determines your happiness in your job. As you do the exercises in this chapter, keep in mind that the insights you gain will serve you outside the workplace as well.

Before you begin your work each day, repeat this affirmation: My work creates value in both my life and the lives of others.

22. I Light Candles Every Day and Surround Myself with Fresh Flowers

Bring feminine energy to your workplace by lighting a candle and bringing in flowers. Lighting a candle, especially at the start of a workday, can function like a ritual or prayer, bringing light and inspiration into your place of business. Similarly, flowers soften, beautify, and bring harmony to almost any environment. By creating more feminine energy where you work, a new, more close-knit atmosphere can take root, barriers can be lowered, and communication and teamwork can become easier.

Creating the Feminine Workplace

Light a candle at the beginning of your workday, either by yourself or inviting your co-workers to join in. If you light the candle alone, write down how this ritual changes the way you look at the beginning of your day. If you do it with others, discuss your reasons for lighting the candle and what difference it can make. If you aren't able to light a candle at work (due to fire restrictions), or in addition to lighting a candle, bring flowers into your work area. Note the change they make in the environment and how they make you feel.

....

....

....

....

....

....

....

....

....

....

....

....

....

....

....

....

....

....

....

Write down other ways you can think of to personalize your work environment.

....
....
....
....
....
....
....
....
....
....
....

22. I Keep My Clutter to a Minimum

Which areas of your life are cluttered? Your office? Your computer desktop? Your calendar? Your bookshelves? Your address book? Your clothes closet? Your car? Your living space? Your mind?

In order to move forward you have to be able to see your way clearly and travel unimpeded. Clutter—both internal and external—must be cleared away. You have to create the right environment to be able to grow.

Clearing My Handbag

The amount of clutter we carry around in our handbags can be alarming. Open yours and empty its contents on the floor. Sort the contents into three piles. List items you absolutely need all the time—like a mobile phone, keys, lipstick, or address book—in the "Keep" column. Put items you use periodically, which you could carry only when you need them, in the "Move" column. Items you never really use go in the "Throw Away" column.

Keep	Move	Throw Away
....	....	....
....	....	....
....	....	....
....	....	....
....	....	....
....	....	....
....	....	....

Put the "Keep" items back in the bag, transfer the "Move" items to the appropriate location, and throw away what is not needed.

My Cluttered Areas

The areas of my life that are cluttered are . . .

....

....

....

....

....

....

The cluttered areas that are holding me back from reaching my full potential are . . .

....

....

....

....

....

....

....

Choose several areas of your life to de-clutter and commit to a date for achieving that goal.

Example: I will de-clutter my filing cabinet by: June 16

I will de-clutter my .... by: ....

I will de-clutter my .... by: ....

I will de-clutter my .... by: ....

I will de-clutter my .... by: ....

I will de-clutter my .... by: ....

I will de-clutter my .... by: ....

I will de-clutter my .... by: ....

I will de-clutter my .... by: ....

23. I Recognize My Gifts and Delegate Other Tasks

Knowing your gifts and shortcomings is a great asset. Honor what you do well and acknowledge others who have different skills. Cultivate and nurture your abilities and talents, but don't be afraid to seek help or delegate tasks and responsibilities to those who have more knowledge and skills than you in certain areas.

Assessing Strengths and Weaknesses

Professionally, my areas of strength are . . .

....

....

....

....

....

Personally, my areas of strength are . . .

....

....

....

....

....

....

....

Areas I need help in are . . .

....

....

....

....

....

....

....

Areas I can offer others help in are . . .

....

....

....

....

....

....

....

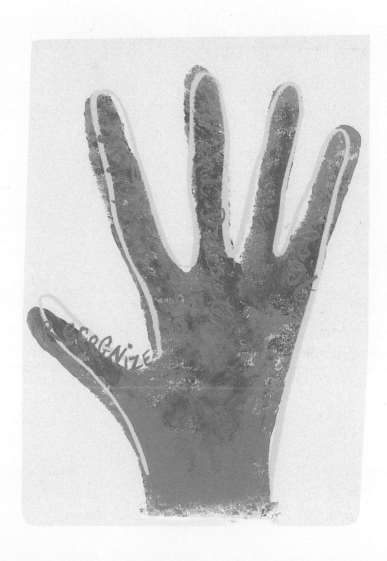

24. I Welcome Mentors and Mentor Others in Return

Mentoring—the sharing of enthusiasm, ideas, experience, and wisdom accumulated through years of effort—is one of the most valuable tools for learning. Without mentors, we may never receive essential knowledge, and by mentoring others we provide a valuable service.

Mutual Mentoring

From the list of "Areas I need help in" from the previous exercise, create a list of people you know who can mentor you or provide you with the assistance you need.

....

....

....

....

....

....

....

....

Contact at least three of the people on this list to determine ways in which they might be able to help you, then ask for that help. Don't be surprised if the people you ask are both flattered and surprised.

Now, from the list of "Areas I can offer help in," research volunteer organizations that can use your expertise, or list people who would benefit from your mentoring. Offer your services to at least one of those people or organizations.

....

....

....

....

....

....

....

....

....

....

....

....

....

....

25. I Smile When Picking Up the Phone

Why smile? Picking up the phone seems like such a trivial act, yet how you carry out this small task reflects the attitude and energy you bring to your job.

We are all sensitive to the positive and negative energy that others project. By consciously radiating positive energy at work and at home, you can often affect the course of a conversation, create a positive outcome, and, most importantly, transform your own state of being.

Accentuating the Positive

Fill in actions of your choice, reframing them in the positive.

Negative	Positive
Example: *I'll try to clean the house.*	*I will clean the house.*
1. If I	I expect ....
2. I ought to	I look forward to ....
3. I could	I can ....
4. I might	I must ....
5. I hope to	I am going to ....

smile when picking up the phone

26. I Look at Difficult Situations from Many Different Perspectives

We all see things through a prism of our own wishes, desires, prejudices, hopes, and moods. And because none of us holds a monopoly on absolute truth and reality, it is important to take into account the opinions and perspectives of others, especially in the workplace. When we do this we gain a greater understanding of the problem at hand and are better able to come up with a fresh solution. If you listen with an open mind, you'll discover everyone has something valuable to contribute.

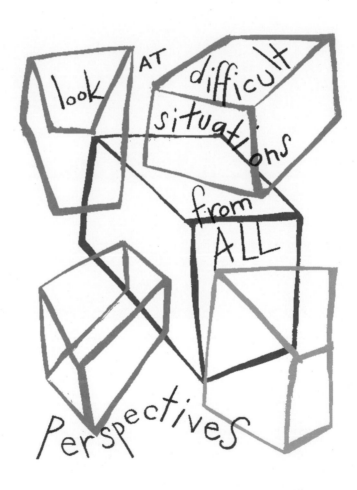

In the Company of Women

Gather three to five of your female colleagues together, and have a discussion on a specific topic about your workplace that interests you all. The topic could be anything from "How would the company be different if women ran it?" to "How could you feminize your workplace?" Be creative; make it interesting and fun.

Write about the discussion. What were the different points of view and perspectives offered? What ideas surprised you? Could you see the validity in the different points of view? What did you learn from the discussion?

....
....
....
....
....
....
....
....
....
....
....
....
....
....
....
....
....
....
....
....
....
....
....
....

27. When I Lose, I Don't Lose the Lesson

When a baby is learning to walk, she falls down many times, but she always gets back up. The baby doesn't know what failure is; she keeps learning her lessons until she finally takes her first steps.

Putting setbacks behind you and moving forward is the key to success, both professionally and personally. When you take action to turn your losses into a lesson, you'll be amazed how your feelings will change.

Winning by Losing

A time when I felt I failed (in my personal life or at work) was . . .

....

....

....

....

....

....

The things that went wrong were . . .

....

....

....

....

....

....

Those things went wrong because . . .

....

....

....

....

....

....

....

The lessons I learned from that situation were . . .

....
....
....
....
....
....
....

I would handle that situation differently today by . . .

....
....
....
....
....
....
....
....
....
....
....
....
....
....
....
....
....
....

When I lose, don't lose the lesson

CONTRIBUTION

Chapter 5

CONTRIBUTION

We all want to live a happy life. But, as I hope this journal has illuminated, achieving happiness does not come from any single source, person, or event, but instead from the variety of choices and actions we take.

For me, one of the greatest sources of happiness is contributing to the lives of others. The old saying "The more you give, the more you get" is absolutely true. When you are selflessly working for a greater good, whether it takes the form of serving others, working to improve your community, or fighting for worldwide change, you begin to tap into a deeper and more profound level of your humanity.

When doing the exercises in this chapter, open yourself to the possibility of giving. By examining your values and considering how best to adhere to those values, you'll be able to determine what kind of service is most appropriate for you.

Making a contribution does not necessarily require taking action on a large scale. There are many ways to contribute, so if a lack of time or money prevents you from doing volunteer work or becoming active in your community, focus on the contributions you can make as an individual, from living responsibly and respecting others to recycling your garbage and using alternative forms of energy.

We all want the world to be a better place, and helping to shape our own futures, and that of our planet, is as important a responsibility as we can have.

28. I Put My Values at the Center of My Life

Challenge yourself to create a holistic life guided by your values and your ethics.
By following your inner moral compass you will always be headed in the right direction.

My Values

Twenty values I believe in are . . .

Examples: *Honesty, Generosity, Openness*

1. ....

2. ....

3. ....

4. ....

5. ....

6. ....

7. ....

8. ....

9. ....

10. ....

11. ....

12. ....

13. ....

14. ....

15. ....

16. ....

17. ....

18. ....

19. ....

20. ....

Put my Values at the center of my life.

INTEGRITY Compassion and LOVE

From that list, the five values that are most important to me are . . .

1. ....

2. ....

3. ....

4. ....

5. ....

Write these five values again in a creative way on a nice sheet of paper, or use your computer and an attractive font to print them out. Put the piece of paper in a prominent place at work, at home, or both, so you can remind yourself daily of how you wish to live your life.

29. I Protect Mother Nature, As She Is the Giver of All Life

The Earth is truly the mother of us all: It sustains our life and surrounds us with beauty. With all the evidence of climate change, air and water pollution, overpopulation, and environmental degradation, it is important to take whatever action we can for our environment. This is important not only for us, but also for our children and our children's children.

My Eco Checklist

- ☐ Do I recycle?
- ☐ Do I walk or bicycle instead of always using a car?
- ☐ Do I try and conserve energy, such as by turning off lights when they're not needed?
- ☐ Do I use alternative forms of energy, such as solar power or wind power?
- ☐ Do I grow some of my own food?
- ☐ Do I compost?
- ☐ Do I use environmentally friendly cleaning products?

List other things you do or could do to live a more environmentally friendly lifestyle.

30. I Change Myself So I Can Change the World

It often seems that a single voice or action couldn't possibly make a difference, but when we change our mindset and recognize the unique power we all have inside of us, we can become catalysts for change. When our individual voices and actions join together, both locally and globally, we can begin to create a new kind of world consciousness. Each and every one of us can make a difference!

Making a Difference

Five things I'd like to see happen to make the world a better place are . . .

....

....

....

....

....

Choose one of the items you listed and write about how you could use your gifts or passions to help make that change happen.

....

....

....

....

....

....

....

....

....

....

Do research to find a group or organization that you can offer your talents, time, and energy to. Once you have made a contribution to the group, come back to this page and write about what you did and how the experience has changed you.

....

....

....

....

....

....

....

....

....

....

....

....

....

....

....

....

31. I Give People More Than They Expect

An unexpected gift usually delights. An unexpected effort does the same. When life is viewed as an opportunity to perform rewarding service, it becomes easy to contribute more at home, at work, and in the world. You'll often find yourself rewarded in equally unexpected ways, too.

Giving More

Ten actions I can take to give more than people expect, whether at home, at work, or in the world, are . . .

....

....

....

....

....

....

....

....

....

....

Pick one of the listed actions and do it. Write about your experience. Was it difficult? Did it make you feel better? Worse? What was the reaction of others to your unexpected effort? What did it do for you?

....

....

....

....

....

....

....

....

....

....
....
....
....
....
....
....
....
....

32. I Recognize My Community and Contribute to It in Every Way I Can

We all need a sense of belonging, of being part of something larger than ourselves. Most of us belong to many different types of communities, some by happenstance (our workplace, the neighborhood where we live) and others by choice (the religious, social, and political groups we belong to). Community is the fabric of human society. Recognize and honor what your communities do for you and the part you play in them.

My Community

To me, "community" means . . .

....

....

....

....

The different communities I belong to are . . .

....

....

....

....

....

Choose one of these communities and describe why it is important to you.

....

....

....

....

....

What I like most about this community is . . .

....

....

....

....

I can contribute more to my community by . . .

....

....

....

....

....

Get five people or so from your community together and begin a dialogue on how you can work together to contribute to your own community or the world.

33. I Remember the Three R's:
Respect for Myself, Respect for Others, and Responsibility for All My Actions

Respecting ourselves means understanding and being grateful for our unique path and the abilities that serve us daily. Respecting others means treating everyone as you would want to be treated. Taking responsibility for your actions requires understanding the effects of everything you do, and never blaming others for choices you have made. When we realize how lucky we are to have this life, it is easy to embrace the Three R's.

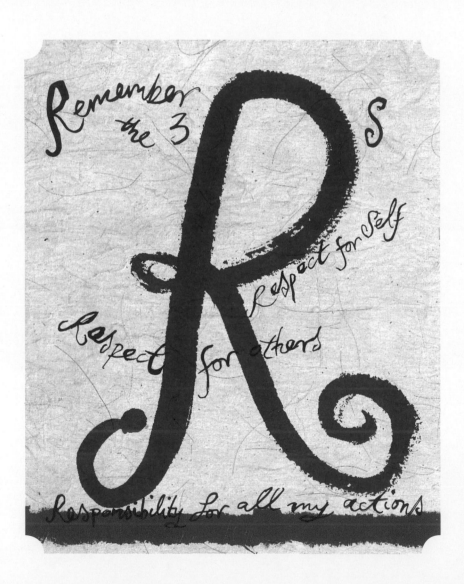

Observing My Day

Go about your day as usual and write about what happens to you, and about your actions.

....
....
....
....
....
....
....
....
....
....
....
....

On the following day, consciously incorporate the Three R's in your actions. Note the difference this makes in your day. Do you feel more positive about your actions? Do other people relate differently to you?

....
....
....
....
....
....
....
....
....
....
....
....
....

THE JOURNEY'S END

Conclusion

THE JOURNEY'S END

All journeys come to an end. All have their challenges, and their rewards. In the pages that follow, look back on the insights you've gained completing this journal and determine how you can integrate them into your life. Then look forward, considering how you can use the essential tools you've gained to help manifest your dreams and be all you were born to be.

34. I Remember That I Am Not Perfect, But I'm Doing the Best I Can

We are all human, and we all have failings and make mistakes. Luckily, though, there is no scorecard in life.

Acceptance is knowing that we did our best and that any mistakes we may have made are only building blocks to our success. Perfection, when achieved, is fleeting. Giving our true and best effort will bring us our ultimate rewards.

Looking Back

Thumb through the pages of this journal and look at the exercises you completed. How open and honest were your answers?

....

....

....

....

....

....

....

....

....

....

....

....

....

....

....

....

....

....

....

....

....

....

Would some of your answers have changed now that you've almost completed your *Bloom* journey?

....

....

....

....

....

....

....

....

....

....

....

....

....

....

....

....

....

....

....

....

....

....

....

....

....

....

....

....

....

What insights about yourself has this journal provided you?

35. I Can Be All I Was Born to Be

There is no reason to hesitate; there are no more excuses to make. What has held you back is behind you. Before you is the bright horizon of unlimited potential. Cast your fears aside and go courageously forward. Never be afraid to be all you were born to be!

Looking Forward

I am going to take the lessons I learned in *Bloom* into my life by . . .

....

....

....

....

....

....

....

....

....

....

....

....

....

....

....

....

....

....

....

....

....

....

....

....

....

I can incorporate the positive image of myself I envisioned in *Bloom* into my life by . . .

The actions I will take to become all I was born to be are . . .

Congratulations! You've completed *Bloom* and are now ready to start a whole new season of your life. As you have proceeded through the exercises and reflective journal entries, you will have noticed how different life has become.

Your enhanced senses and ability to enjoy the moment will have improved the quality of your life tremendously. By living your life in a conscious manner, taking responsibility for your actions, and creating the time for quiet reflection, you have blossomed into the glorious woman you were always meant to be.

Use the pages that follow to continue your journey, and reflect upon your experiences.

Keep on gardening,

REFERENCES AND RESOURCES

I have selected just a few of my favorite books and Web sites that have inspired me during the writing of *Bloom*. I hope you will find them as useful as I have.

Personal Growth

Hay, Louise L. *The Power Is Within You*. Hay House/Eden Grove, 1991.

Jayanti, B. K. *God's Healing Power: How Meditation Can Help Transform Your Life*. Michael Joseph/Penguin Group, 2002.

Mountain Dreamer, Oriah. *The Invitation*. HarperSanFrancisco, 1999.

Roth, Gabrielle and John London. *Maps to Ecstasy: Teachings of an Urban Shaman*. Mandala/HarperCollins, 1989.

Steinem, Gloria. *Revolution from Within: A Book of Self-Esteem*. Little, Brown & Co., 1992.

Williamson, Marianne. *A Woman's Worth*. Random House, 1993.

Well-Being

Curtis, Susan, and Romy Fraser. *Natural Healing for Women: Caring for Yourself with Herbs, Homoeopathy, and Essential Oils.* Thorsons, 1992.

Hay, Louise L. *You Can Heal Your Life.* Hay House, 1999.

Horrigan, Bonnie J. *Red Moon Passage: The Power and Wisdom of Menopause.* Random House, 1996.

Kenton, Leslie. *Age Power: The Revolutionary Path to Natural High-Tech Rejuvenation.* Vermilion/Random House, 2002.

Linn, Denise. *Secrets and Mysteries: The Glory and Pleasure of Being a Woman.* Hay House, 2002.

Nahmad, Claire. *Earth Magic: A Wisewoman's Guide to Herbal, Astrological, and Other Folk Remedies.* Destiny/Inner Traditions, 1993.

Northrup, Christiane, M.D. *Women's Bodies, Women's Wisdom.* Bantam, 1994, 1998, 2002.

Roth, Gabrielle. *Sweat Your Prayers: Movement as Spiritual Practice.* Putnam/Penguin, 1998.

Neal's Yard Remedies
www.nealsyardremedies.com

Optimum Health Institute
www.optimumhealth.org

Gabrielle Roth
www.ravenrecording.com

Relationships

Anand, Margo. *The Art of Sexual Ecstasy.* Tarcher/ Penguin, 1989.

Bly, Robert, and Marion Woodman. *The Maiden King: The Reunion of Masculine and Feminine.* Henry Holt, 1998.

Deida, David. *Intimate Communication: Awakening Your Sexual Essence.* Health Communications, 1995.

Gray, John, Ph.D. *Men Are From Mars, Women Are From Venus.* HarperCollins, 1992.

Hendricks, Gay, Ph.D, and Kathlyn Hendricks, Ph.D. *Conscious Loving: The Journey to Co-Commitment.* Bantam, 1990.

Peck, M. Scott. *The Road Less Traveled.* Simon & Schuster, 1978 (US); Hutchinson & Co., 1983 (UK).

David Deida
www.deida.info

John Gray
www.marsvenus.com

Parenthood.com
www.parenthood.com

M. Scott Peck
www.mscottpeck.com

Chuck Spezzano
www.psychologyofvision.com

Tantra.com
www.tantra.com

Work

Boyle, David. *Funny Money: In Search of Alternative Cash.*
    HarperCollins UK, 1999.

Franks, Lynne. *The Seed Handbook: The Feminine Way to Create Business.*
    Hay House, 2005.

Hawken, Paul. *The Ecology of Commerce: A Declaration of Sustainability.*
    Harper Business, 1994.

Helgesen, Sally. *The Web of Inclusion.* Currency/Doubleday, 1995.

Twist, Lynne. *The Soul of Money: Transforming Your Relationship with Money
    and Life.* W.W. Norton, 2003.

SEED
    www.seednetwork.com

Women in Business International
    www.forwomeninbusiness.com

Black Career Women
    www.bcw.org

Business for Social Responsibility
    www.bsr.org

National Association of Women Business Owners (NAWBO)
    www.nawbo.org

Social Venture Network (US)
    www.svn.org

Contribution

H.H. the Dalai Lama. *Compassion or Competition: A Discussion on Human Values in Business and Economics.* Spirit in Business, 2002.

Eisler, Riane. *The Chalice and the Blade.* HarperSanFrancisco, 1988, 1990.

Estrich, Susan. *Sex and Power.* Riverhead Books/Penguin Putnam, 2000, 2001.

Gladwell, Malcolm. *The Tipping Point: How Little Things Can Make a Big Difference.* Little, Brown & Co., 2000.

Handy, Charles. *The Age of Unreason.* Harvard Business School Press, 1989.

Hawken, Paul, Amory Lovins, and L. Hunter Lovins. *Natural Capitalism: Creating the Next Industrial Revolution.* Little, Brown, 1999.

Klein, Naomi. *No Logo: No Space, No Choice, No Jobs.* Picador, 2000.

Perkins, John. *Confessions of an Economic Hit Man.* Berrett-Koehler, 2004.

Roddick, Anita. *Take It Personally: How Globalization Affects You and Powerful Ways to Challenge It.* Conari Press, 2001.

Adbusters
www.adbusters.org

Amnesty International
www.amnesty.org

Greenpeace
www.greenpeace.org

UNESCO
www.unesco.org

UNIFEM
www.unifem.org

World Wildlife Fund
www.wwf.org

Friends of the Earth
www.foe.co.uk

Human Rights Watch
www.hrw.org

Oxfam
www.oxfam.org.uk

Rocky Mountain Institute
www.rmi.org

Sierra Club
www.sierraclub.org

The Journey's End

Franks, Lynne. *Grow: The Modern Woman's Handbook*. Hay House, 2004.

Franks, Lynne. *Plant Seeds and Pick the Blooms Deck.* Chronicle Books, 2005.

Houston, Jean. *A Passion for the Possible: A Guide to Realizing Your True Potential.* HarperSanFrancisco, 1997.

Matthews, Caitlin. *In Search of Woman's Passionate Soul.* Element Books, 1997.

Murray, Elizabeth. *Cultivating Sacred Space: Gardening for the Soul.* Pomegranate, 1998.

Tolle, Eckhart. *A New Earth: Awakening to Your Life's Purpose.* Dutton Adult/Penguin, 2005.

Williamson, Marianne. *A Return to Love: Reflections on the Principles of A Course in Miracles.* Aquarian Press/HarperCollins, 1992.

About Lynne Franks

Author, teacher, and groundbreaking businesswoman Lynne Franks inspires women throughout the world with her books, speaking engagements, seminars, and workshops. Among her noted works are *The Seed Handbook: The Feminine Way to Create Business*, *Grow: The Modern Woman's Handbook*, and the *Plant Seeds and Pick the Blooms Deck.*

Her SEED seminars and educational programs have been expanded into an international virtual network for women entrepreneurs (www.seed network.com), as well as a series of women's enterprise learning programs accessible to women of all ages, ethnicities, and social backgrounds.

Lynne conducts in-depth workshops in the United Kingdom and special retreats in Mallorca, Spain. More information about Lynne can be found at www.lynnefranks.com.